THE HUMAN BODY

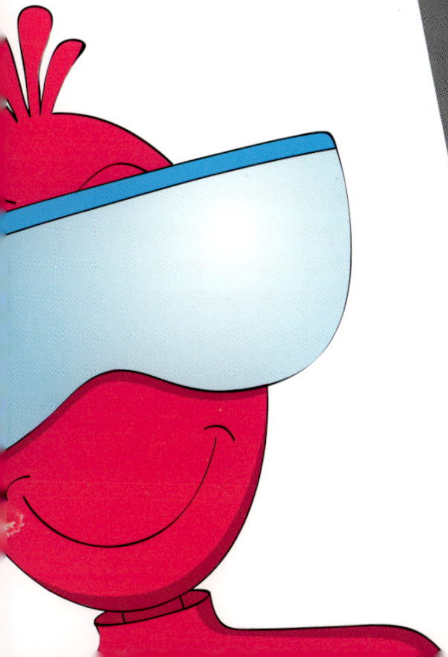

KINGFISHER
NEW YORK

Copyright © Kingfisher 2012
Published in the United States by Kingfisher,
175 Fifth Ave., New York, NY 10010
Kingfisher is an imprint of Macmillan
Children's Books, London.
All rights reserved.

Distributed in the U.S. and Canada by Macmillan,
175 Fifth Ave., New York, NY 10010

Library of Congress Cataloging-in-Publication data
has been applied for.

ISBN: 978-0-7534-6977-4

Kingfisher books are available for special promotions and premiums. For details contact: Special Markets Department, Macmillan, 175 Fifth Ave., New York, NY 10010.

For more information, please visit
www.kingfisherbooks.com

Printed in China
10 9 8 7 6 5 4 3 2 1
1TR/0512/LFG/140MA

Written and Illustrated by Dynamo Ltd.
Concept by Jo Connor

WHAT'S IN THIS BOOK?

THE HUMAN BODY...

6	WHAT IS INSIDE MY BODY?
7	DO BABIES HAVE THE SAME THINGS INSIDE THEM AS ME?
8	WHY DOESN'T EVERYONE LOOK THE SAME?
9	HOW TALL WILL I GROW?
10	WHY DO I BLINK?
11	WHY DO I CRY?
12	WHAT ARE EYEBROWS FOR?
13	IS ANYONE HAIRY ALL OVER?
14	WHY DO I GET HUNGRY?
15	WHY DO I GET THIRSTY?
16	WHY DO I POOP?
17	WHAT IS PEE?
18	WHY DOES MY STOMACH GROWL?

19	WHY DO I BURP?	43	WHY DO PEOPLE SNORE?
20	WHY DO PEOPLE FART?	44	WHY DOES MY NOSE RUN?
21	WHAT IS MY TONGUE FOR?	45	WHAT IS A SNEEZE?
22	WHY DO CUTS BLEED?	46	ARE ALL BELLYBUTTONS THE SAME?
23	WHAT IS A SCAB FOR?	47	WHAT MAKES ME HICCUP?
24	WHO HAS SKIN COVERED IN HOLES?	48	WHY DO SOME PEOPLE WEAR GLASSES?
25	WHAT ARE FRECKLES?	49	WHAT DOES "COLORBLIND" MEAN?
26	WHEN DO MOLES LIVE ON PEOPLE?	50	WHY DO I NEED TO GET MY NAILS CUT?
27	WHAT IS A SCAR?	51	WHY DOES HAIR FALL OUT?
28	WHEN DO I NEED TO WEAR SUNSCREEN?	52	WHY DO EARS MAKE WAX?
29	WHY DO I GET GOOSE BUMPS WHEN IT'S COLD?	53	WHAT WOBBLES INSIDE MY EAR?
30	WHY DOES TICKLING MAKE ME GIGGLE?	54	HOW QUICKLY DOES MY HEART BEAT?
31	WHY DO I NEED TO BATHE?	55	WHY DO I SOMETIMES GET OUT OF BREATH?
32	WHAT ARE MY BONES MADE OF?	56	QUICK-QUIZ QUESTIONS
33	HOW DO MY ARMS AND LEGS BEND?	58	QUICK-QUIZ ANSWERS
34	WHY CAN'T I TURN MY FOOT BACKWARD?	60	TRICKY WORDS
35	WHAT WOULD HAPPEN IF I BROKE A BONE?	62	WHERE TO FIND STUFF
36	WHAT IS MY SMALLEST BONE?	64	FAREWELL
37	WHAT IS MY BIGGEST BONE?		
38	WHY SHOULD I BRUSH MY TEETH?		
39	WHY DO TEETH GET WOBBLY?		
40	WHY DO I YAWN?		
41	WHAT IS SLEEP FOR?		
42	WHAT AM I DOING WHEN I SLEEP?		

HAVE YOU EVER WONDERED WHY... OR WHAT... OR WHEN?

It's natural to wonder about the world around us. It's a very complicated and surprising place sometimes. And you'll never understand what is going on around you unless you ask yourself a question every now and then.

We have investigated the human body to collect as many tricky questions as we could find about how your body works...

...and we also found the answers for you!

We now invite you to come with us on an exploration of the human body so that we can show you all of the answers we have discovered.

We also thought it might be fun to see how much of this shiny new knowledge you can remember—so at the back of the book, on pages 56 and 57, you'll find some Quick-Quiz questions to test you. It's not as scary as it sounds—we promise it will be fun. (And, besides, we've given you all of the answers on pages 58 and 59.)

While we were searching for all of those answers, we found out some other pretty interesting things, too. We wrote them all down on these panels—so you can memorize these facts and impress your friends!

Did you know . . .
Your heart beats about 100,000 times a day—that's roughly 36,500,000 beats per year!

Are you ready for this big adventure?

Then let's go!

WHAT IS INSIDE MY BODY?

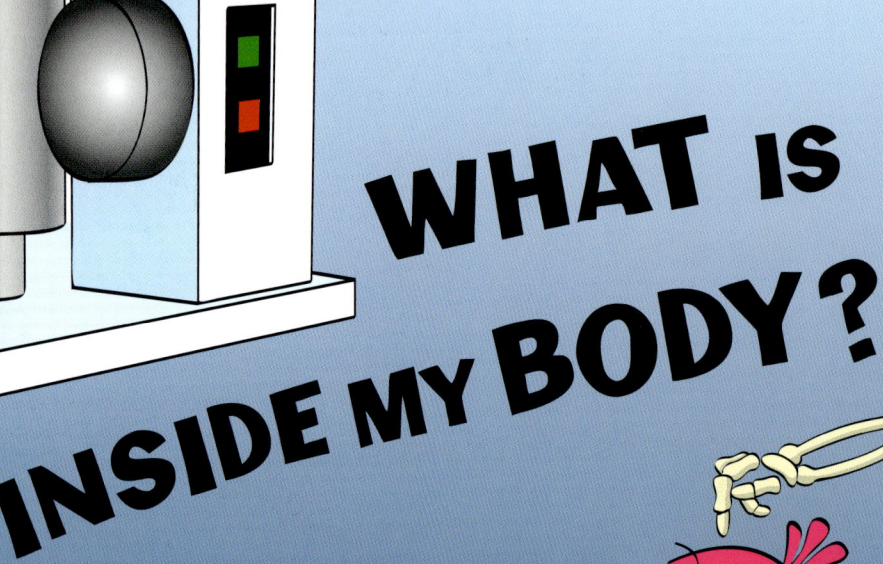

Did you know...

Worn-out cells inside your body die off and get replaced by new ones all the time.

Inside your body there are many soft parts, such as your heart and stomach. These are protected by a skeleton made of hard bones. Every part of your body, hard or soft, is made of tiny building blocks called cells. You have trillions of them!

WHY DOESN'T EVERYONE LOOK THE SAME?

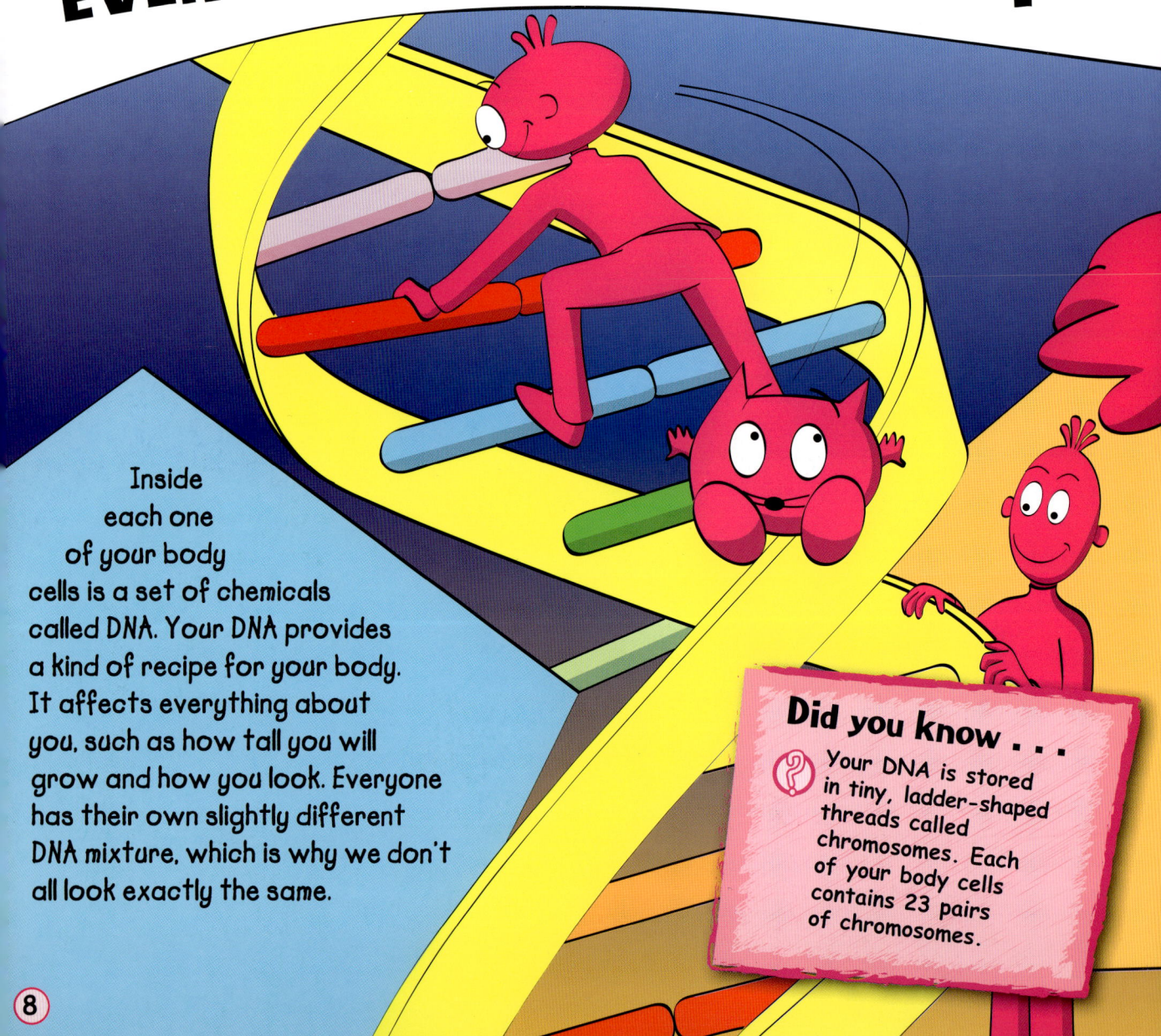

Inside each one of your body cells is a set of chemicals called DNA. Your DNA provides a kind of recipe for your body. It affects everything about you, such as how tall you will grow and how you look. Everyone has their own slightly different DNA mixture, which is why we don't all look exactly the same.

Did you know . . .
Your DNA is stored in tiny, ladder-shaped threads called chromosomes. Each of your body cells contains 23 pairs of chromosomes.

HOW TALL WILL I GROW?

Did you know . . .

Your hair grows faster than anything else on your body. It grows about four nanometers every second—that is about 0.4 millimeters each day.

How tall you become depends on your DNA, and the recipe for your DNA comes from your family. If you have a tall mom or dad, you have more chance of growing tall, too. But growing tall also depends on how healthy you are. Eating healthy food will help your body grow as much as it can.

WHY DO I BLINK?

You blink to stop your eyes from drying out. Your top eyelids are lined with tiny body parts called glands that make a liquid to coat your eyes. When you blink, you spread the liquid over your eyeballs. Blinking also cleans your eyes, like a windshield wiper cleaning a car's windshield.

Did you know . . .

Children and grownups blink between 10 and 15 times a minute, but babies blink less.

Your top eyelids produce a liquid that cleans your eyes, but if you get upset, they suddenly start to make more liquid. Nobody knows exactly why this happens, but it may be your body's way of helping you calm down. Tears contain a chemical called "prolactin" that scientists think might have a calming effect.

WHY DO I CRY?

Did you know . . .

Your body automatically makes tears to try to clean your eyes if they are irritated by something, such as the chemicals that waft up from an onion when it is cut.

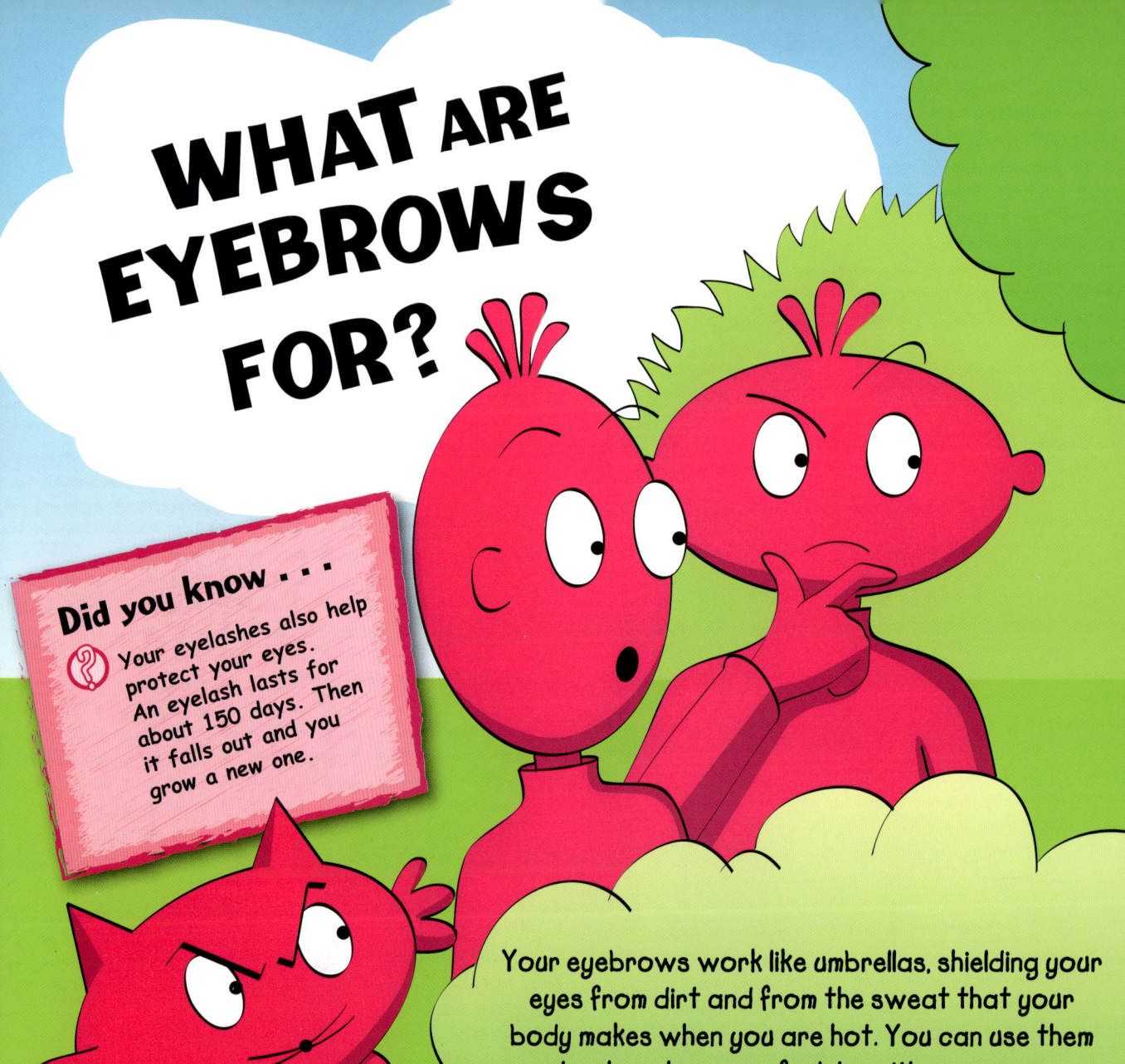

IS ANYONE HAIRY ALL OVER?

We have many tiny hairs all over our skin to help protect it and keep it warm. Nobody is hairy all over, though. We don't have hair on the soles of our feet, the palms of our hands, our eyelids, or our lips.

Did you know . . .
Humans have a scent, like most animals do, but it is very faint and we do not normally notice it. Our tiny hairs might help keep it on our skin.

WHY DO I GET HUNGRY?

Your body uses food as fuel and to keep you healthy. When you need more, your brain sends you a signal that your belly feels empty. Without food, your body would eventually stop working, just as a car would stop working if it ran out of gas.

Did you know...

If you did not eat enough food, you would become thin, weak, and sick.

WHY DO I GET THIRSTY?

Did you know . . .

Splish splash! About two thirds of your body is made up of water.

The feeling of thirstiness is your body's way of telling you that you need more water. Water stops your body from drying out, and your body uses it to do jobs such as making blood or helping mash up food in your stomach. You need to drink water every day to replace what you have used.

WHAT IS PEE?

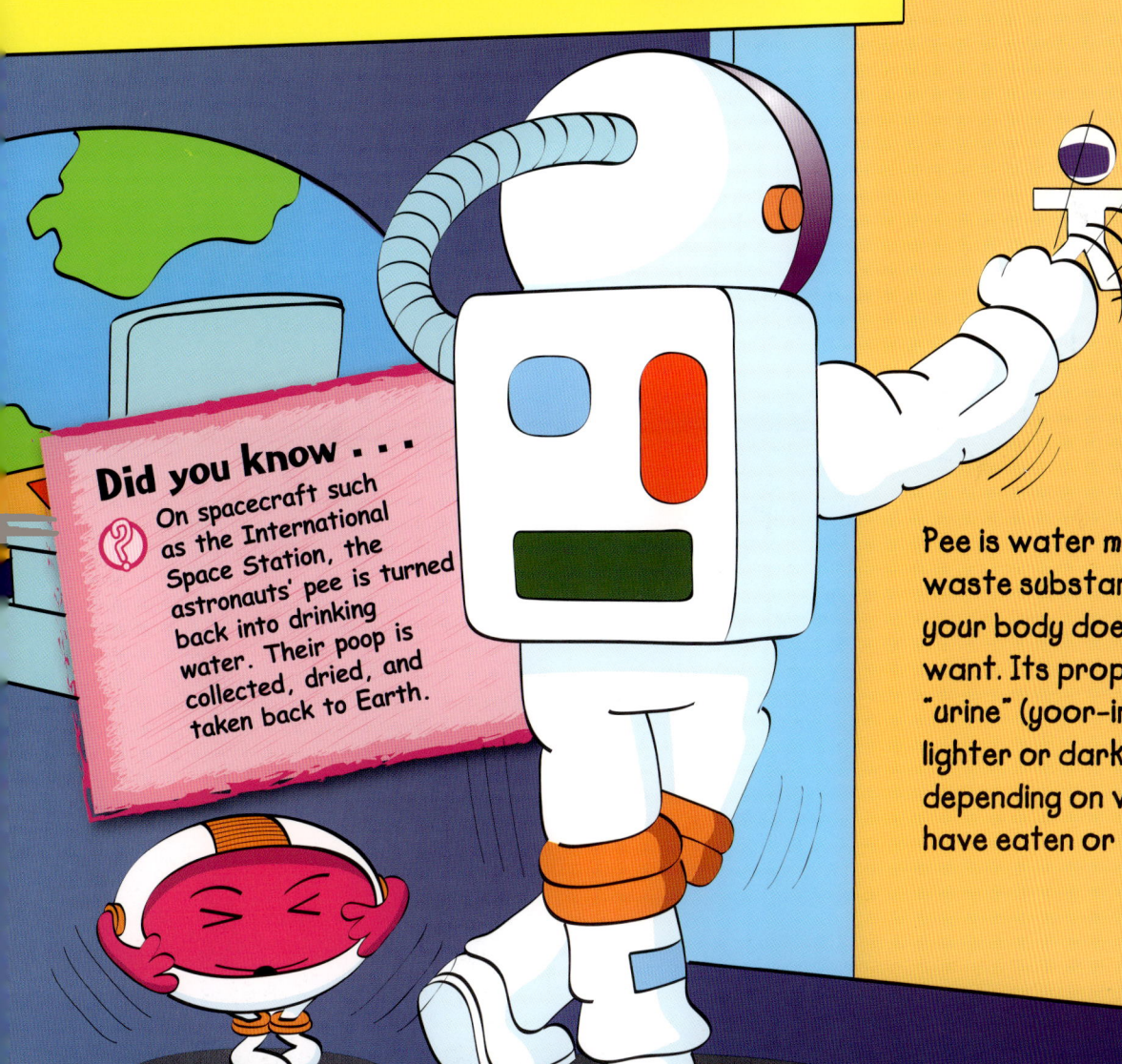

Did you know... On spacecraft such as the International Space Station, the astronauts' pee is turned back into drinking water. Their poop is collected, dried, and taken back to Earth.

Pee is water mixed with waste substances that your body does not want. Its proper name is "urine" (yoor-in). It can be lighter or darker in color, depending on what you have eaten or drunk.

17

WHAT IS MY TONGUE FOR?

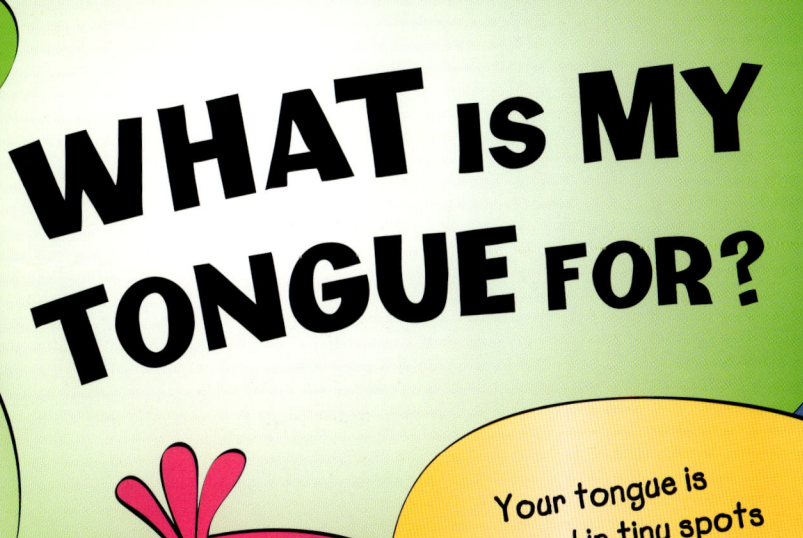

Did you know...

Your tongue allows you to speak clearly, helping you form certain sounds and words.

Your tongue is covered in tiny spots called taste buds. These can sense different tastes, and they help you figure out what is good to eat and what is not. You taste sweet things at the front of your tongue, sour things at the sides, bitterness at the back, and saltiness at the front and sides.

WHY DO CUTS BLEED?

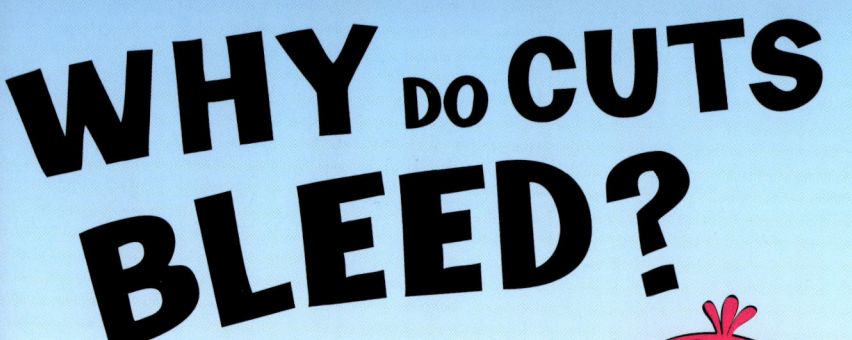

Your body has blood flowing around inside it, helping keep you healthy. It flows through thin tubes called blood vessels. Your skin has tiny blood vessels running underneath it. So if you cut your skin, blood leaks out from the damaged vessels.

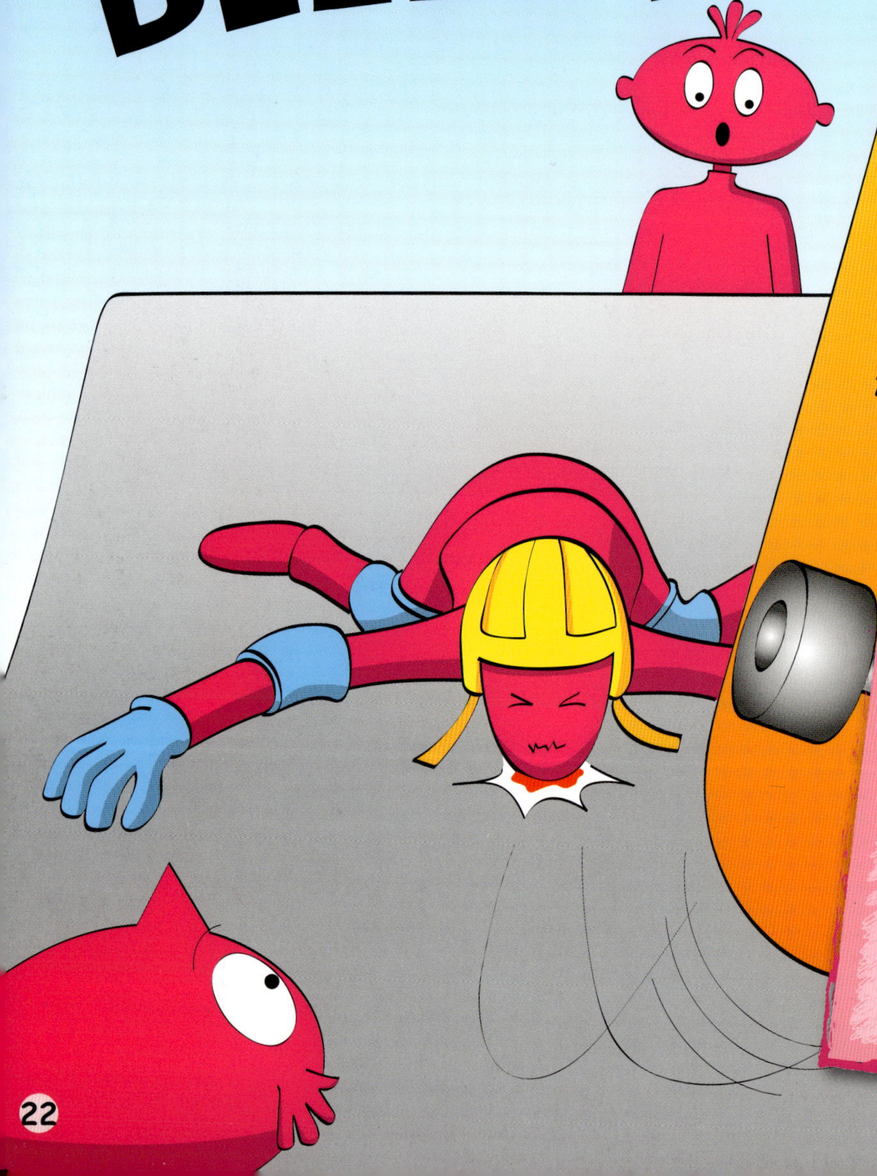

Did you know . . .

If you bump yourself, you can damage the blood vessels under your skin without cutting yourself. Blood leaks out under the skin's surface, forming a bruise.

22

WHAT IS A SCAB FOR?

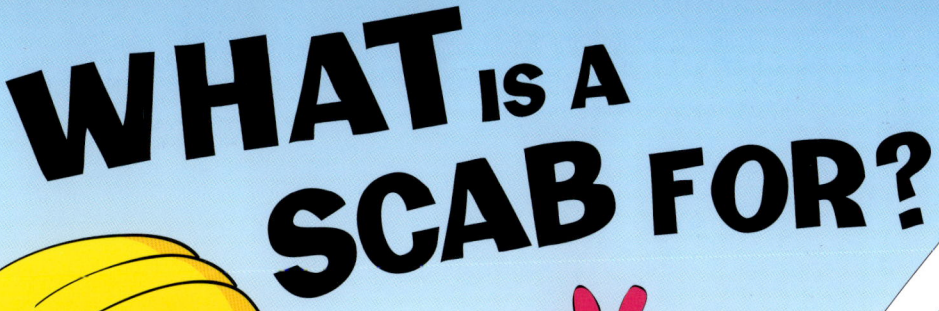

Did you know . . .
A scab will fall off when the skin's surface has healed. Try not to pull it off before it is ready. Leave it to do its job!

When blood leaks out of a cut, tiny blood cells called platelets clump together to make a sticky plug called a clot. They eventually plug the hole and the clot becomes a scab that protects the cut while it heals. Underneath, your body gets busy making new skin cells.

WHO HAS SKIN COVERED IN HOLES?

Did you know . . .

Your hair and skin is coated in oil, made under your skin. The oil makes your skin and hair waterproof.

Everybody's skin is covered in tiny holes called pores. If you get hot, your body makes sweat, a salty liquid that leaks out through the pores. It evaporates (disappears into the air), which helps make you feel cooler.

WHAT ARE FRECKLES?

Did you know . . .

Freckles don't do any harm, and sometimes they fade away over time. Fair-skinned people can get more freckles if they spend time outside in the sun.

Your skin has "pigment cells" that contain the chemicals that give your skin its color. Freckles are little clusters of pigment cells in the uppermost layer of your skin. They are most easily seen on people with fair skin.

WHY DOES TICKLING MAKE ME GIGGLE?

Nobody knows for sure why tickling makes us laugh. It could be because your brain is surprised! Your skin contains many tiny nerve endings that sense touch. Some nerve endings are supersensitive to light touching. They may signal to the brain extra fast, and your brain reacts to the surprise by making you laugh.

Did you know . . .

You cannot tickle yourself. Your brain does not react to your own touch in the same way as it reacts to somebody else's touch. Perhaps this is because you cannot surprise it!

WHY DO I NEED TO BATHE?

Did you know . . .

As children grow into adults, their skin starts to make more oil and sweat.

Your skin produces an oily coating to keep you waterproof and salty sweat to keep you cool. If you did not wash these off sometimes, more and more dirt and bacteria would stick to the oil and sweat. You would soon start to smell and would eventually become unhealthy.

WHAT ARE MY BONES MADE OF?

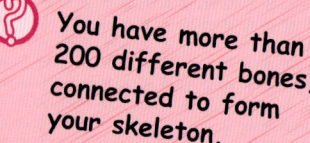

Did you know...
You have more than 200 different bones, connected to form your skeleton.

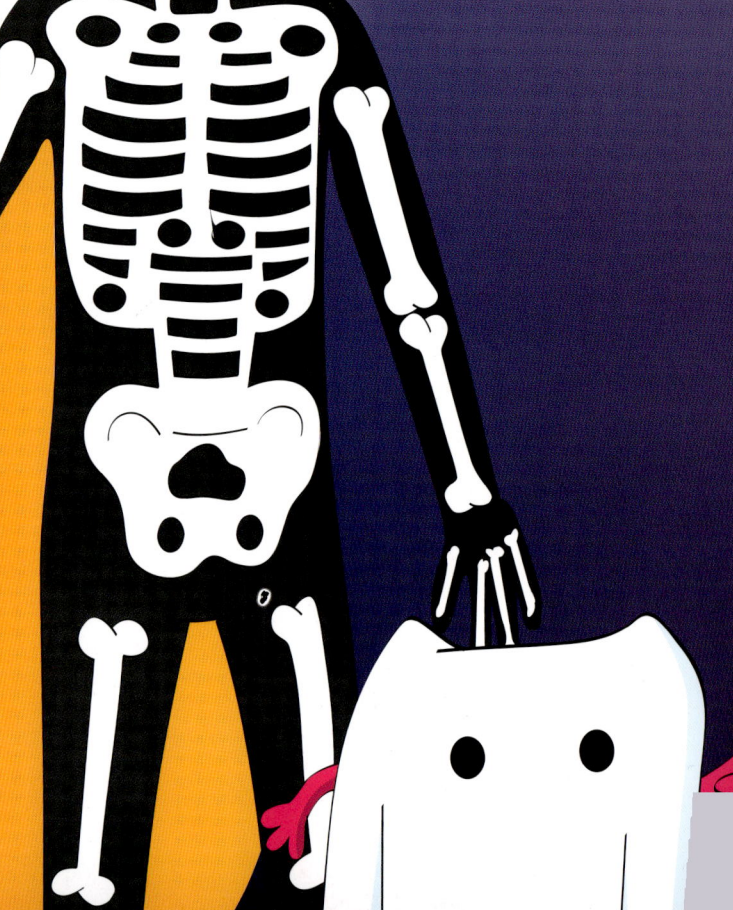

Your bones are a mixture of stretchy material and strong, hard material. They have many tiny holes through the middle, like a sponge, which makes them lightweight. They make up a framework inside you that holds the shape of your body and protects your insides.

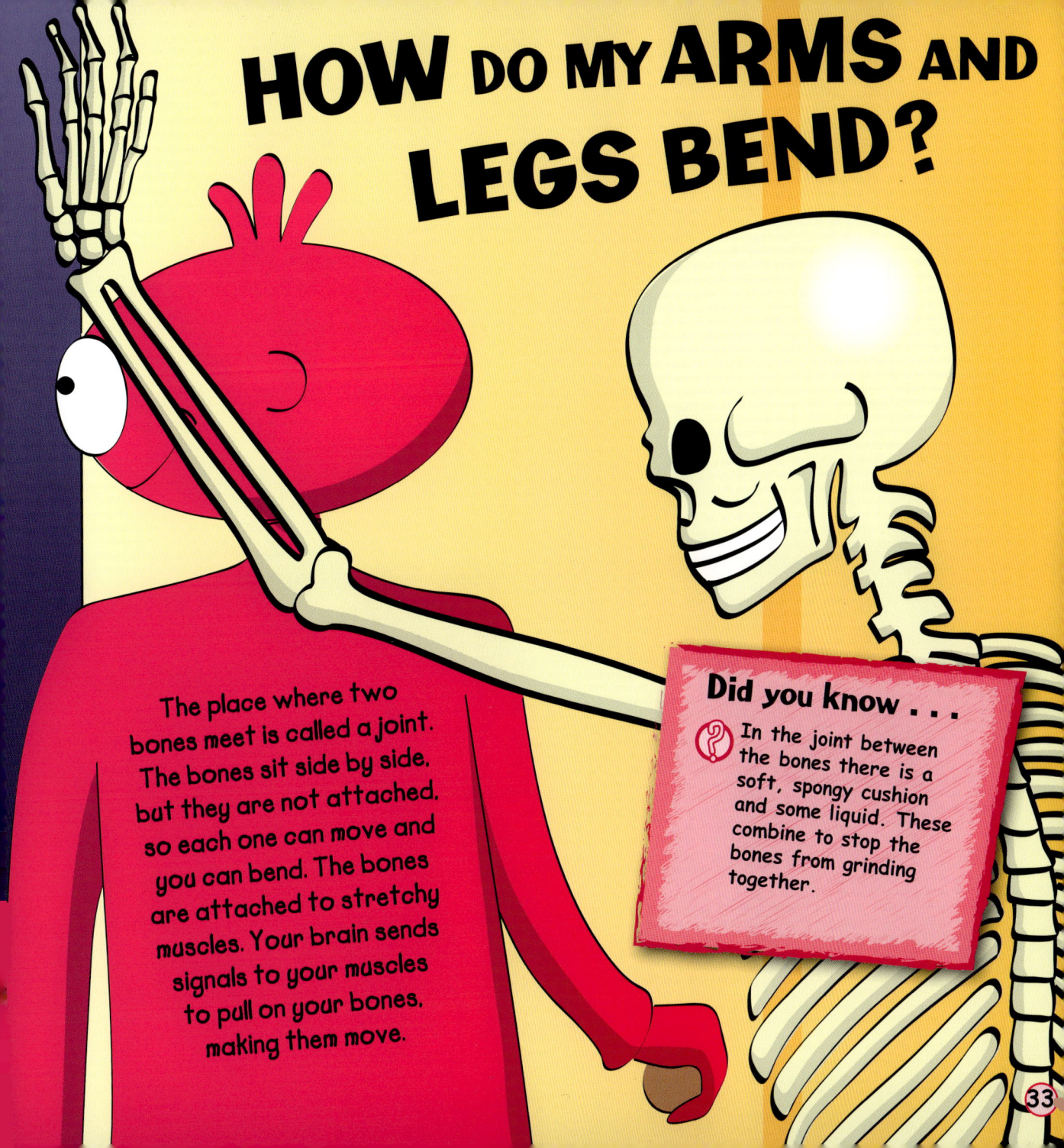

WHAT IS MY SMALLEST BONE?

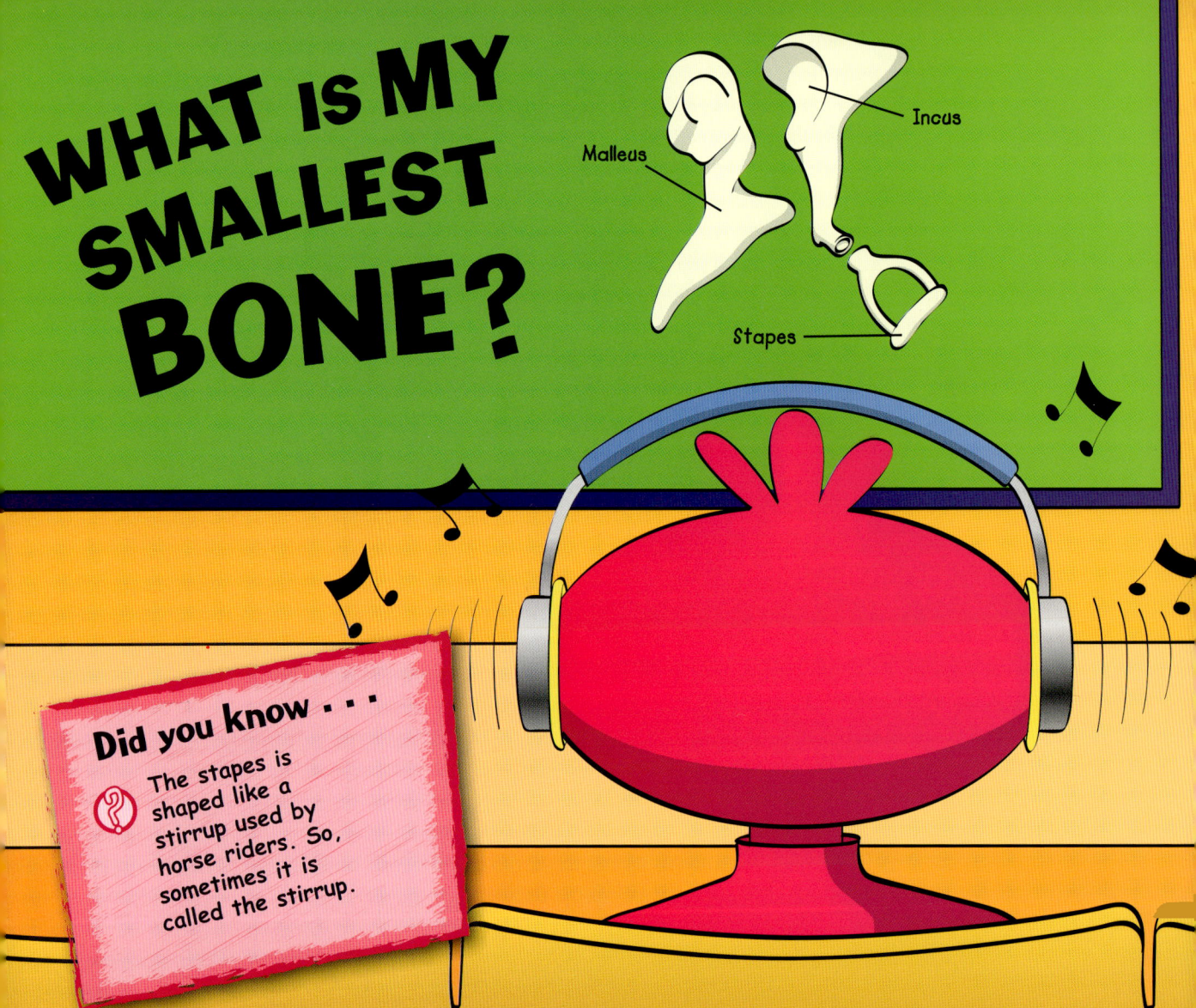

Malleus
Incus
Stapes

Did you know . . .
The stapes is shaped like a stirrup used by horse riders. So, sometimes it is called the stirrup.

The smallest bone in your body is inside your ear. It is called the stapes (stay-peas), and it is about three millimeters long. Sound waves make it wobble. It passes the wobbling on to other parts of your ear, where there are nerve endings that send messages to your brain. Your brain can tell from the messages what sound you are hearing.

WHAT IS MY BIGGEST BONE?

Did you know . . .

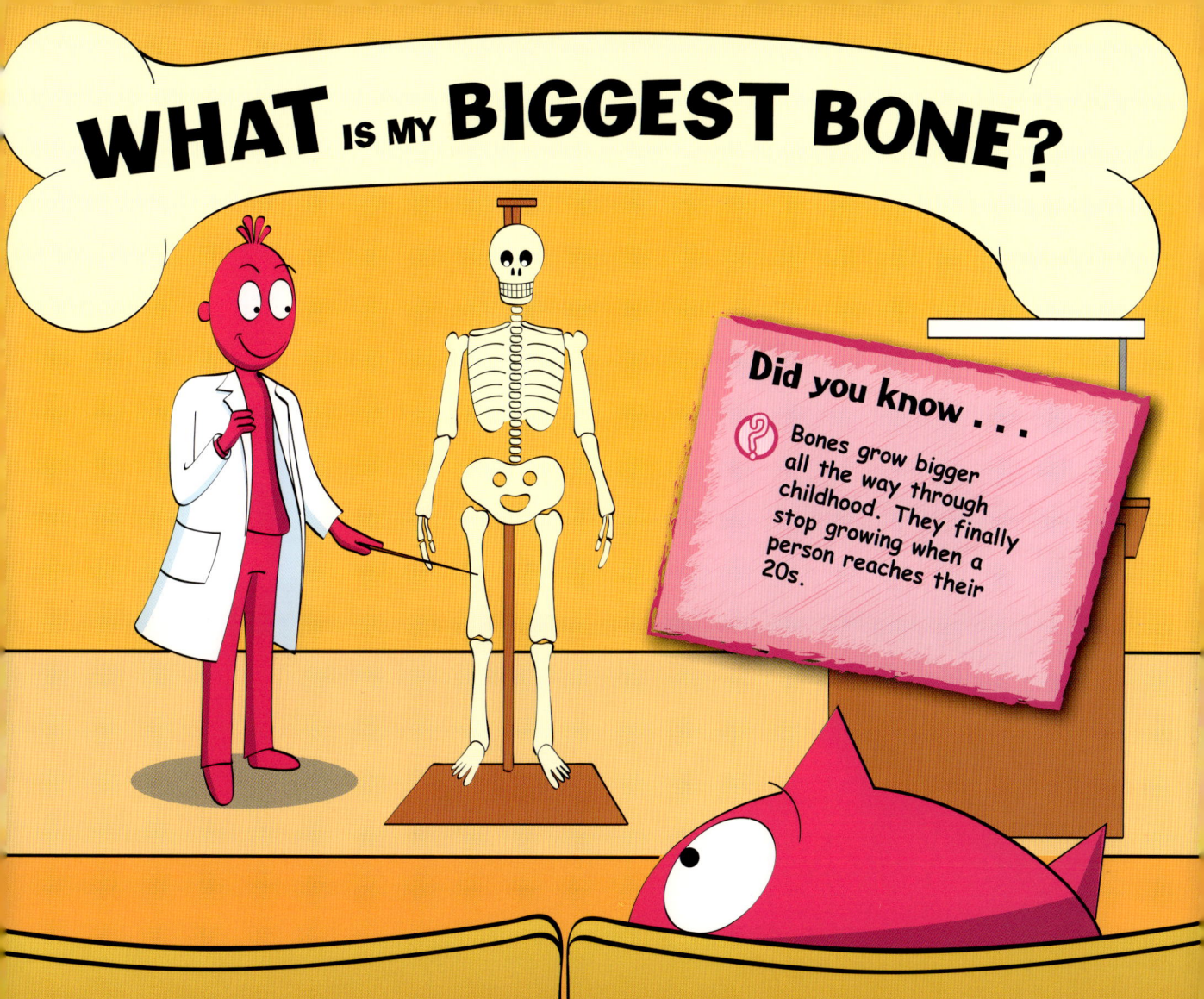

Bones grow bigger all the way through childhood. They finally stop growing when a person reaches their 20s.

The longest, strongest bone in the body is the femur (fee-mer), also called the thighbone. It is fixed between your pelvis (where your waist and hips are) and your knee. It has strong muscles attached to it to help you move your legs.

WHY SHOULD I BRUSH MY TEETH?

Did you know...

Before toothpaste was invented, people brushed their teeth with all sorts of things, including ashes, lemon juice, and ground-up chalk.

When you eat, particles (tiny pieces) of food and drinks stick to your teeth. Left on your teeth, they turn into chemicals called acids that slowly dissolve your teeth and make them rot. Regularly brushing your teeth helps get rid of the acids.

WHY DO TEETH GET WOBBLY?

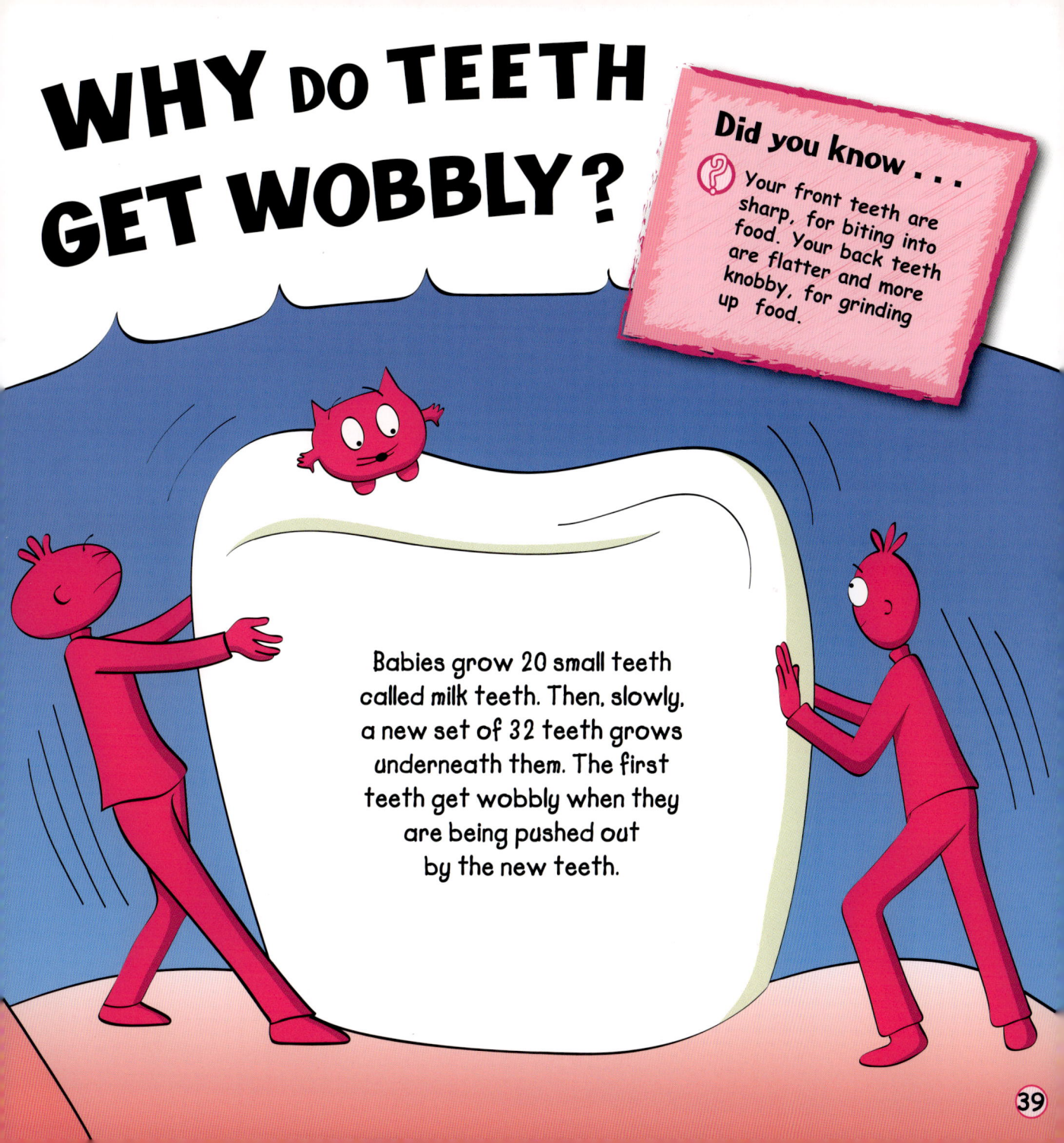

Did you know... Your front teeth are sharp, for biting into food. Your back teeth are flatter and more knobby, for grinding up food.

Babies grow 20 small teeth called milk teeth. Then, slowly, a new set of 32 teeth grows underneath them. The first teeth get wobbly when they are being pushed out by the new teeth.

WHY DO I YAWN?

Did you know . . .

Yawning spreads fast! If one person yawns, anyone who sees them tends to yawn soon afterward. Nobody knows why.

Nobody knows for sure why we yawn. It could be because we breathe less deeply than normal when we are tired, bored, or just waking up. So yawning could simply be our body's way of making us breathe better or more deeply.

WHAT IS SLEEP FOR?

Sleep gives all of your body parts a much-needed rest. Without sleep, you would soon be too tired and worn out to even think properly, and you would start to get angry and clumsy.

Did you know...

Growing up is tiring! Babies sleep for around 14 hours a day. Children need about ten hours of sleep a day, and adults generally need less.

WHAT AM I DOING WHEN I SLEEP?

Did you know...

In total, people spend about one third of their lives asleep.

While you are asleep, your body relaxes. Your breathing slows down and your heartbeat slows, too. Meanwhile, your brain gets the chance to sort and store information from the day. Nobody knows for sure why people dream when they are asleep. It could be your brain's way of sorting out what you have been thinking.

WHY DO PEOPLE SNORE?

Did you know . . .

Almost one half of all adults tend to snore when they sleep. Children sometimes snore, too.

People may make snoring noises while they sleep, if the back of their throat vibrates (wobbles) in a different way to how it does when they are awake. This might be because someone's nose is stuffed up or the back of their throat is slightly blocked.

WHY DOES MY NOSE RUN?

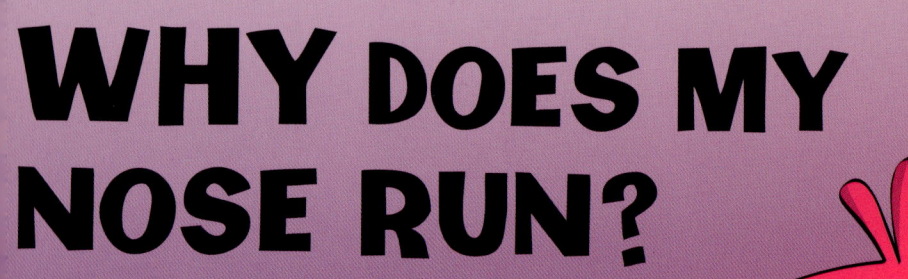

Your nose makes mucus (mew-cus), a gooey slime that is also called snot. It lines the inside of your nose and catches dirt and germs before they get the chance to go inside your lungs. Your nose makes extra mucus for protection if it is irritated—perhaps by dust or by the germs you get if you catch a cold.

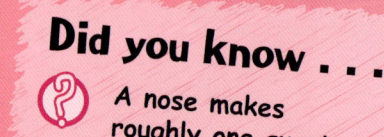

Did you know . . .

A nose makes roughly one quart (1L) of mucus every day. That's the same as about three or four mugs of mucus!

WHAT IS A SNEEZE?

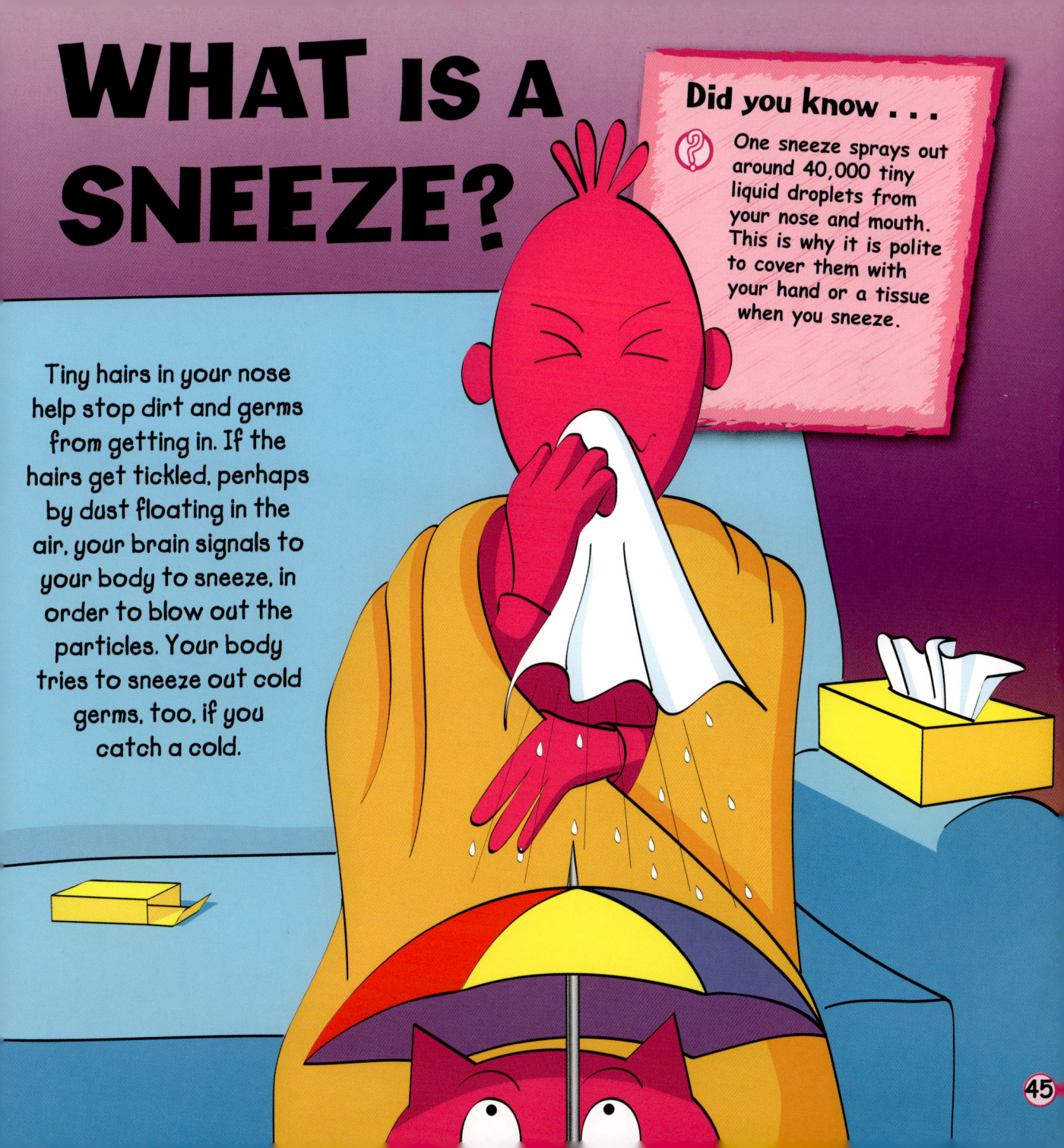

Did you know . . .

One sneeze sprays out around 40,000 tiny liquid droplets from your nose and mouth. This is why it is polite to cover them with your hand or a tissue when you sneeze.

Tiny hairs in your nose help stop dirt and germs from getting in. If the hairs get tickled, perhaps by dust floating in the air, your brain signals to your body to sneeze, in order to blow out the particles. Your body tries to sneeze out cold germs, too, if you catch a cold.

45

ARE ALL BELLYBUTTONS THE SAME?

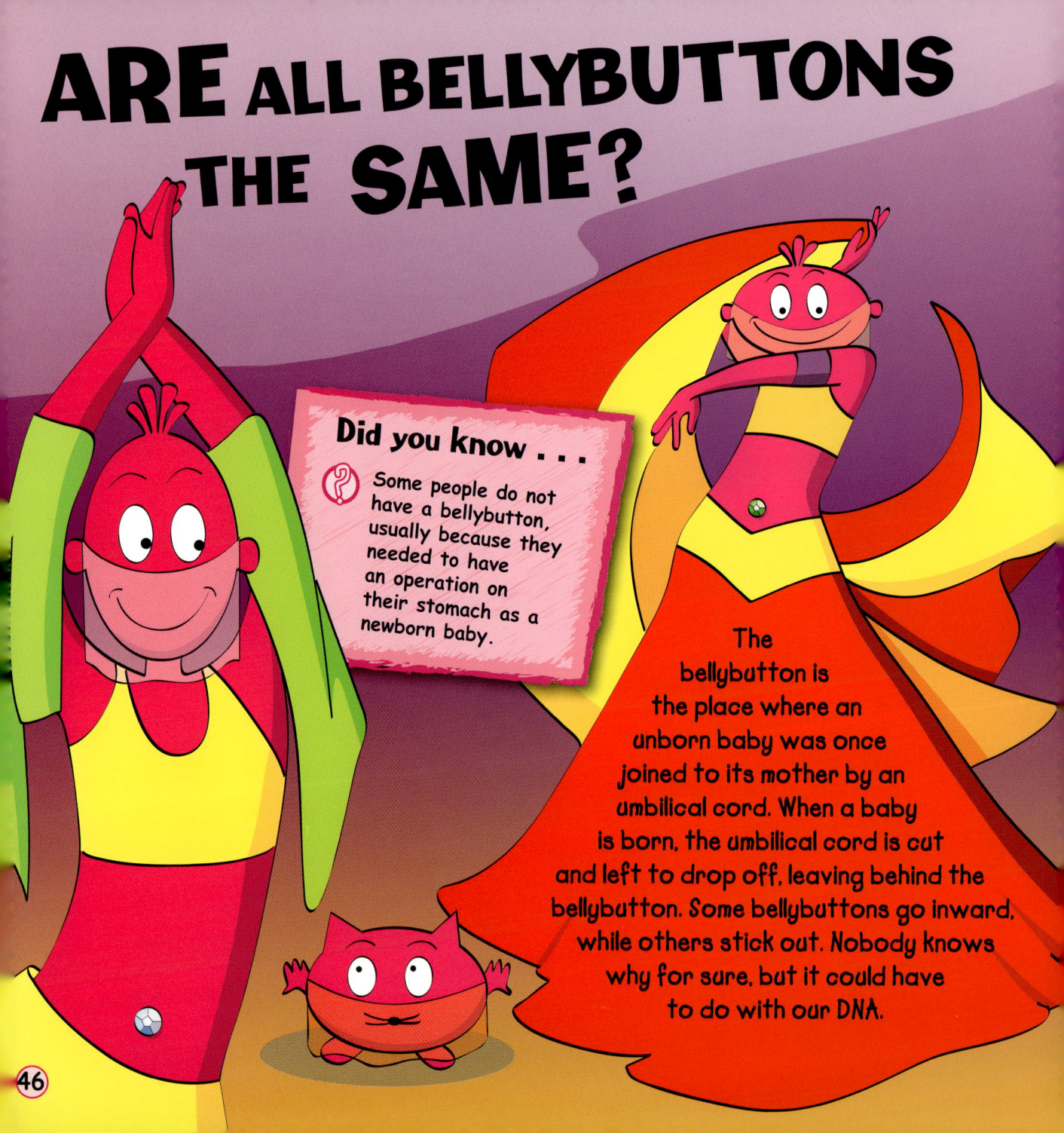

Did you know . . .

Some people do not have a bellybutton, usually because they needed to have an operation on their stomach as a newborn baby.

The bellybutton is the place where an unborn baby was once joined to its mother by an umbilical cord. When a baby is born, the umbilical cord is cut and left to drop off, leaving behind the bellybutton. Some bellybuttons go inward, while others stick out. Nobody knows why for sure, but it could have to do with our DNA.

WHAT MAKES ME HICCUP?

Inside your chest, below your lungs, there is a large wall of muscle called the diaphragm (dye-a-fram). It moves up and down automatically when you breathe, but sometimes it gets out of control, and this is when you get the hiccups. The sound of hiccups is the noise made by part of your throat closing quickly.

Did you know . . .

Even unborn babies can get the hiccups!

WHY DO SOME PEOPLE WEAR GLASSES?

Did you know...
Shortsighted people cannot see very far away. Farsighted people are not able to properly see things when they are close up.

An eye works by collecting light and focusing it into a picture on the retina—the sensitive layer at the back of the eye. If your eyes cannot properly focus light, you do not see clearly. Glasses are extra lenses that help eyes focus better.

WHAT DOES "COLORBLIND" MEAN?

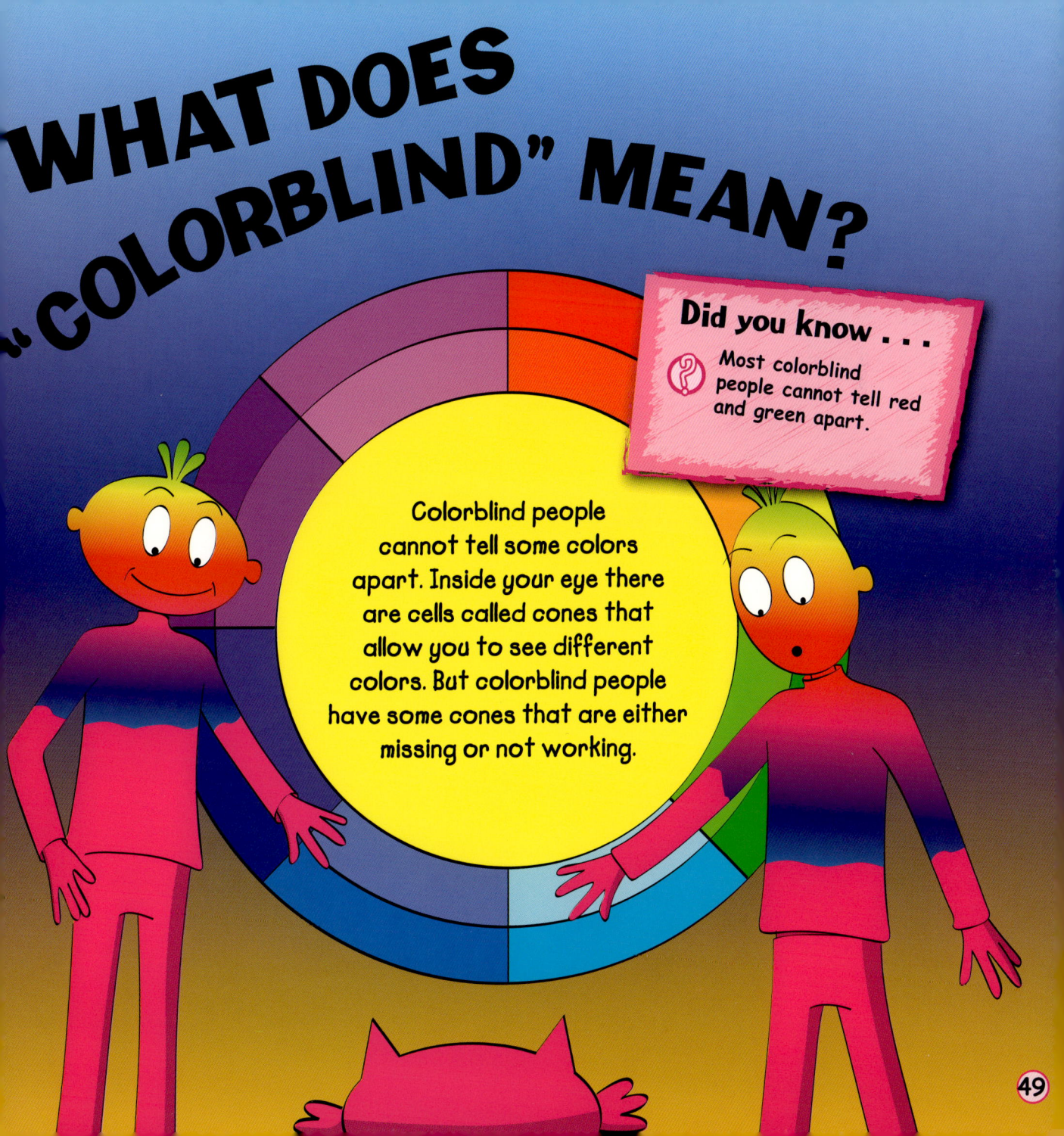

Did you know . . .
Most colorblind people cannot tell red and green apart.

Colorblind people cannot tell some colors apart. Inside your eye there are cells called cones that allow you to see different colors. But colorblind people have some cones that are either missing or not working.

49

WHY DO I NEED TO GET MY NAILS CUT?

Did you know . . .

Fingernails grow three to four times faster than toenails!

Your nails are made of a type of hard protein called keratin. They protect the ends of your fingers and toes. They grow all the time, replacing nails that are worn out or broken. Nails grow roughly 2 in. (5cm) a year. If you never cut them, they would grow superlong and curly, like twigs on the ends of your fingers!

WHY DOES HAIR FALL OUT?

Did you know...

Hair is made of dead body cells. This is why it does not hurt when you get your hair cut.

It is normal to lose between 50 and 100 hairs a day, mostly when you brush or wash your hair. You have about 100,000 hairs on your head. Each hair grows for about two years, growing from its root inside the skin. When it finally falls out, a new hair grows in its place.

WHY DO EARS MAKE WAX?

Did you know...

The medical name for earwax is cerumen (se-roo-mun).

Your body makes a gooey wax in a tube called the ear canal, inside the entrance to your ear. The wax keeps out dirt particles and infections and stops your ears from getting dry and itchy. It is made from body oil, sweat, and dead skin flakes. It sounds disgusting, but it does not harm you. In fact, earwax does a very important job!

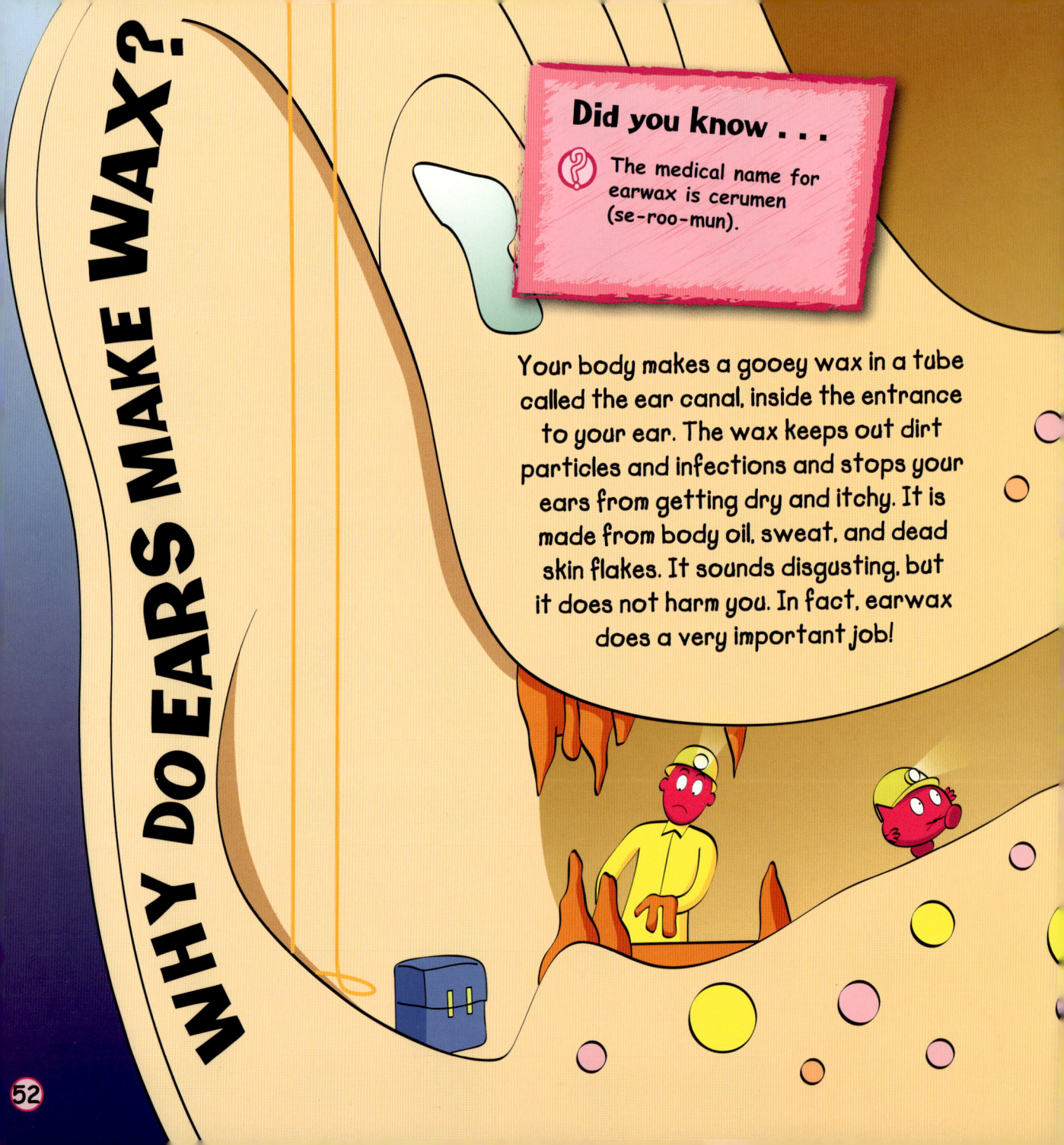

WHAT WOBBLES INSIDE MY EAR?

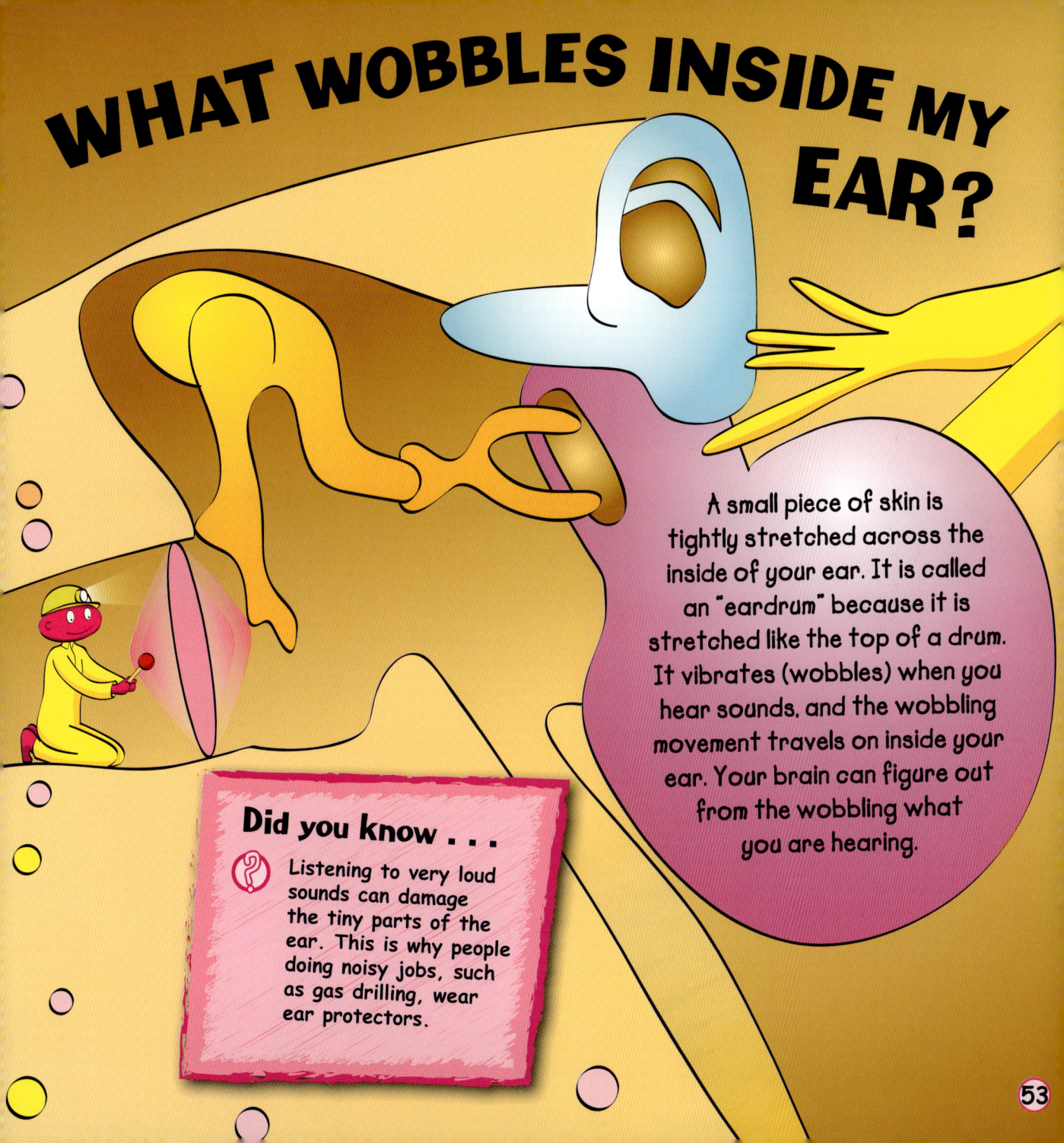

A small piece of skin is tightly stretched across the inside of your ear. It is called an "eardrum" because it is stretched like the top of a drum. It vibrates (wobbles) when you hear sounds, and the wobbling movement travels on inside your ear. Your brain can figure out from the wobbling what you are hearing.

Did you know . . .

Listening to very loud sounds can damage the tiny parts of the ear. This is why people doing noisy jobs, such as gas drilling, wear ear protectors.

HOW QUICKLY DOES MY HEART BEAT?

When you are resting, your heart beats between 70 and 100 times a minute. The heart is a big muscle that pumps blood around your body. Blood gives you the oxygen you need and takes away waste from your body cells. Your heart beats faster when you exercise, ensuring that your body has enough oxygen.

Did you know . . .

You can feel your heart beating by taking your pulse. Press lightly on the inside of your wrist to feel your blood being pumped around your body. Each beat you feel is your heart contracting (squeezing).

WHY DO I SOMETIMES GET OUT OF BREATH?

Did you know . . .

If you get in shape and do plenty of exercise, your lungs will get stronger and better at their job—and you will feel less breathless when your body works hard.

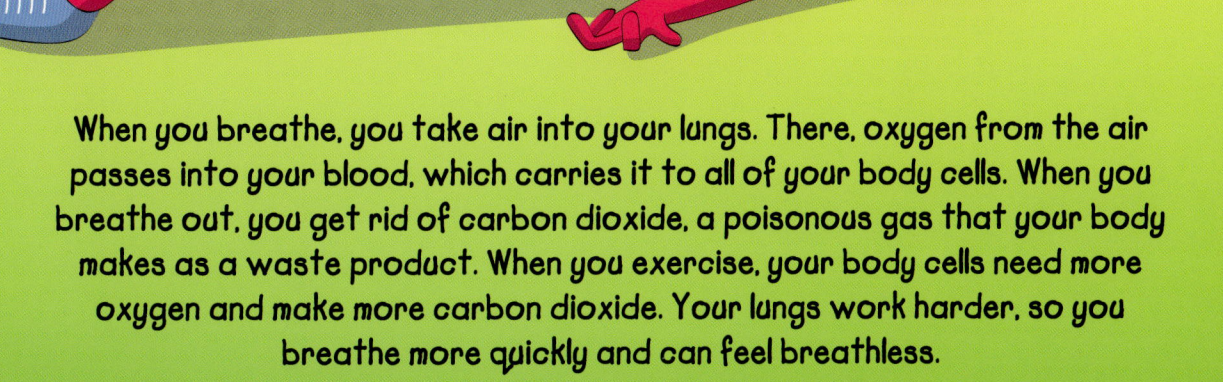

When you breathe, you take air into your lungs. There, oxygen from the air passes into your blood, which carries it to all of your body cells. When you breathe out, you get rid of carbon dioxide, a poisonous gas that your body makes as a waste product. When you exercise, your body cells need more oxygen and make more carbon dioxide. Your lungs work harder, so you breathe more quickly and can feel breathless.

QUICK-QUIZ QUESTIONS

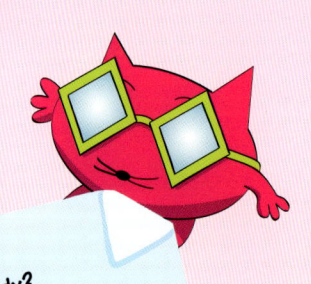

1. How many cells are in your body?
   a) thousands b) millions c) trillions

2. Your eyes grow bigger as you get older. True or false?

3. Where would you find a chromogome in your body?

4. Your hair grows faster than anything else on your body. True or false?

5. Do you blink to stop your eyes from drying out or to push away water from your eyes?

6. Name a place on your body where you don't have hair.

7. How much of your body is made of water?

8. The digestive system is the system of the body that makes you breathe. True or false?

9. Does your stomach growl loudest when it is empty or full?

10. Does drinking soda cure burping?

11. What type of taste do you sense at the front of your tongue—sweet or sour?

12. Your body has many thin tubes that carry blood around. What are they called? a) blood ways b) blood vessels c) heart tubes

13. Does your skin have holes in it?

14. Most adults have around 1,000 moles. True or false?

15. Is a lot of sunlight good or bad for the skin?

16. Adults sweat more than children. True or false?

17. Are bones heavy or light?

18. Your bones can rebuild themselves. True or false?

19. Where is your smallest bone?

20. What are a baby's first teeth called?

21. When you are asleep, your breathing slows down. True or false?

22. Do all bellybuttons look the same?

23. Colorblind people cannot see any colors. True or false?

24. What are nails made of?

25. How many times a minute does your heart beat?

QUICK-QUIZ ANSWERS

1. c) trillions
2. False. Your eyes stay the same size your whole life.
3. Chromosomes are found in your cells.
4. True.
5. You blink to stop your eyes from drying out.
6. The soles of the feet, palms of the hands, eyelids, lips.
7. Two thirds of your body is water.
8. False. The digestive system processes food.
9. Your stomach growls loudest when it is empty.
10. No. Drinking soda makes burping worse.
11. Sweet.

12. b) Blood vessels.

13. Yes—they are called pores.

14. False. Most adults have between 10 and 40 moles.

15. Too much sun is bad for the skin.
16. True.

17. Bones are light.

18. True.

19. In your ear.
20. Milk teeth.

21. True.
22. No. There are "innies" and "outies."

23. False. They cannot tell some colors apart.

24. Nails are made of keratin.
25. Your heart beats between 70 and 100 times a minute.

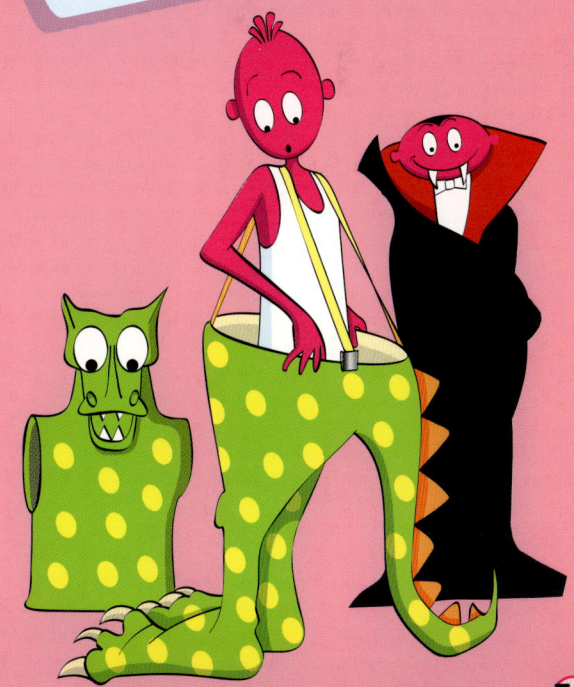

TRICKY WORDS

BACTERIA
Tiny organisms (life forms) that are too small to be seen without a microscope. Some are harmless, but some can make people sick.

BLOOD VESSEL
A narrow tube that carries blood around your body.

CARBON DIOXIDE
A gas, poisonous to humans, that is created by your body cells as they do their work.

CELL
A tiny building block that makes up every living thing.

CHROMOSOME
A tiny ladder-shaped thread in every body cell where DNA is stored.

DIAPHRAGM
A dome-shaped area of muscle that helps you breathe in and out.

DIGESTIVE SYSTEM
The system of your body that takes nutrients from food and gets rid of any unwanted stuff in food.

DNA
A set of chemicals found in every cell. DNA controls how the body looks and works.

EAR CANAL
A tube inside the entrance to the ear.

EARDRUM
A tiny piece of skin that is tightly stretched across the inside of the ear.

FEMUR
The biggest bone in the body, located in the top part of the leg.

GLAND
A body part that makes a substance such as earwax, tears, or skin oil.

JOINT
A place where two bones meet each other.

LUNGS
Two bag-shaped body parts inside your chest. Air is drawn inside the lungs when you inhale (breathe in).

MUCUS
Gooey slime that lines the inside of the nose, catching dirt and infections before they get inside the body.

MUSCLE
Stretchy material attached to bones. Muscles contract (squeeze) and relax to make bones move.

NERVE ENDING
A tiny body part that can sense things such as touch or heat.

OXYGEN
A gas that your body needs to help it work. Oxygen is in the air that we breathe in.

PARTICLE
A very tiny piece of something.

PELVIS
The bone in between the base of your back and the top of your legs.

PLATELET
A cell that floats in the blood. Its job is to stop bleeding by clumping together to block cuts.

PORE
A tiny hole on the skin.

RETINA
The sensitive surface at the back of the eye.

SKELETON
The framework of bones that protects your soft insides and holds your body shape.

STAPES
The tiniest bone in the body, in the ear.

TASTE BUD
A tiny spot on the tongue that can sense different types of tastes.

UMBILICAL CORD
The cord that attaches an unborn baby to its mother.

URINE
The proper name for pee—water mixed with waste substances that your body needs to get rid of.

VIBRATE
To wobble very rapidly. Parts of the ear vibrate when they hear sounds.

WHERE TO FIND STUFF

B
babies 7, 10, 39, 41, 46, 47
bacteria 31, 60
bellybuttons 46
bleeding 22, 23
blinking 10
blood 22, 23, 54
blood vessels 22, 60
bones 6, 32, 33, 35, 36, 37
breathing 40, 42, 55
burping 19

C
carbon dioxide 55, 60
cells 6, 8, 23, 25, 26, 27, 28, 35, 49, 51, 54, 55, 60, 61
chromosomes 8, 60
colorblindness 49
cuts 22, 23, 27

D
diaphragm 47, 60
digestive system 16, 18, 19, 20, 60
DNA 8, 46, 60
dreaming 42

E
eardrums 53, 60
ears 36, 52, 53, 60
earwax 52
eyebrows 12
eyelashes 12
eyelids 10, 11
eyes 7, 10, 11, 12, 48, 49

F
farting 20
femurs 37, 60
food 14
freckles 25

G
giggling 30
glands 10, 60
glasses 48
goose bumps 29

H
hair 9, 13, 51
hearing 36, 53
heart 6, 54
height 9
hiccups 47
hunger 14

62

JL
joints 33, 34, 60
lungs 55, 60

M
moles 26
mucus 44, 60
muscles 33, 37, 61

N
nails 50
nerves 30, 36, 61
nose 44, 45

O
oil 24, 31, 52
oxygen 54, 55, 61

PQR
pelvis 37, 61
pigment 25, 26
platelets 23, 61
pores 24, 61
prolactin 11
pulse 54
retinas 48, 61

S
scabs 23
scars 27
scent 13
shivering 29
skeleton 6, 61
skin 13, 22, 23, 24, 25, 26, 27, 28, 29
sleeping 41, 42, 43
sneezing 45
snoring 43
stapes 36, 61
stomach 6, 15, 18
sunburn 28
sunscreen 28
sweat 24, 31, 52

T
taste buds 61
tears 11
teeth 38, 39
thirst 15
tickling 30
tongue 21

U
umbilical cord 46, 61
urine 17, 61

WXYZ
washing 31
water 15
yawning 40

Wow! What an amazing journey! We hope you had as much fun as we did and learned many new things. Who knew there was so much to discover about the human body? Here are some other exciting books in which you'll find more to explore:

The Book of . . . Dinosaurs
The Book of . . . How?
The Book of . . . What?
The Book of . . . Where?
The Book of . . . Which?
The Book of . . . Who?
The Book of . . . Why?

Look out for these great books! "Who" knows "what" we'll discover . . .
See you soon!